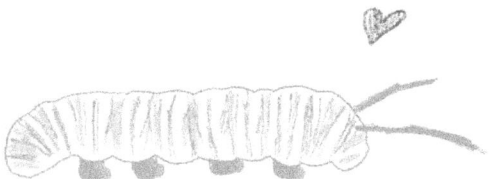

BUTTERFLY NET

Emily Parent

Butterfly Net
by Emily Parent

ISBN: 979-8-9914745-0-4

Original cover art by Maria Ananieva. Oil on Paper.
MariaAnanieva.com

For permissions, inquiries, or more information, please
visit emilyparent.com, or connect over email at
contact@emilyparent.com.

*For my mother, who lovingly watched
and waited as her children chased butterflies.*

Table of Contents

Part 1

Saving My Life	6
Clean Kill	8
Abandon Ship	9
The Rules	11
Summer in Silicon Valley	13
ADHD	14
String Lights	19
On Mothers and Moths	20
Summer in Atlanta	21
Dear Professor	22
Top Bunk	26
Butterfly Net	27
Caesura	31

Part 2

When Winter Breaks   37

I Don't Miss You   39

Poet Girl's Prayer   41

I Forgive You, Stranger   42

Spilt   43

Breath   44

I Forgive You, Lover   45

Half Moon Bay   46

The Vintage Shop   47

Neighbor Boy   49

What If This is All We Get?   51

Dear Governor   54

Building A Nest   57

Savasana   58

Pretty Things   59

Hey Emily—
do you have a second
to chat?
KEEP WORKING!
Enjoy this mug instead of a raise!

Part 1

SAVING MY LIFE

I've started to Notice each day.

The clouds are a buttery
color of cream
dough-like and tuffet-y
ambling
boundless on

                blue.

True,
I have tried many times
to measure my life
in check-marks
of pen-ink — calories, dollars, pass-

                fail —

to gather a fragmented
day in cupped-hands
and place it with
fear on a

                scale

                How
I'd pray to the wandering needle:
I would beg her to mend
this unseemly and endless
directionless spend of my

                soul.

Now.
I Notice. My breath, sweetly:

Ebb. Flow. Repeat.
Drifting indulgently
cloud-like.
Ebullient.

                                        Full.

(The debt to myself — I forgave.)

CLEAN KILL

She put on mascara the morning she ended my life.

I think how she probably smirked as she leaned on the sink,
parted her lips and rolled up her eyes,
sharpened her lashes to points with a rarely used wand

wild-eyed, pondering how I would gape like a soft-bellied fish
when she tugged up my line and sliced me down long-ways
to scoop out my quivering guts with her steeple-point nails.

One hour later we sat down to chat
and sterile as counter-tops, cold as white light, she made a
precision-incision with words meant to flay —

"Your role is no longer required here. Have a nice day!"

The meeting was quick and I lurched out the door like a ghost: sheet-white
and heavy with unfinished business echoing halls in my wake.
No funeral eulogies — memory piled in a meeting room sent up in flames.

I hear now they scornfully mutter my name
and survey with ire my dead rotting unassigned tasks.
I swear on occasion I feel curses placed on my grave.

And those who did love me are mournful and waiting
with anticipation for her to get dressed up again - rabid and ready to
claw out their pretty red hearts with a saccharine grin.

ABANDON SHIP

You tried to be someone who put on a suit
Who sacrificed hours pursuing the fruit
of salary, raises, and slow steady growth
while under the shoes of the people you loathe.
You called yourself stable — that siren-like myth.
In truth there is no such stability with
a tech job, non-profit, or government work
nor finance, nor healthcare — there always will lurk

the office-place politics, some bottom line,
or aging directors who hate when you shine.
So even if you are the picture of grace
and with every play you've presented an ace
They'll tell you that this was just never a fit
or moan that the budget has taken a hit
and leave you marooned on a hot sandy beach
Then wave goodbye grinning as you gasp and reach

for reasons this happened, but you'll come up short,
and in the next paper you'll read a report
of how you went rabid and had to be shot.
Then you'll take a breath…

... and you'll notice you're not
the version of you that you thought you would be.
And that stable job never did set you free.
So, shaking, you wade through the sea of unknown
with hope that the ink-and-star sky guides you home.

The salty seawater is not like you feared
and now that you're moving you find your mind cleared.
That ship had been awful! The job made you sick.
And every gray day they would force you to pick
between standing still as they leaned to punch down
Or stepping to meet them and holding your ground.
You'd spent so much time on your knees cleaning dirt
that you'd come to ignore just how bad your knees hurt.

Now on the blue waves you begin to collect
wet wood for a raft, and you come to suspect
that given some time you can build your own boat.
And with some self-trust you will learn how to float
across the horizon to find a new land.
Then with your soft beating heart in your hand
you'll find it: a stable place ground in the earth.
Now dig yourself up and embrace what you're worth!

THE RULES

She clearly did not know The Rules
since it was her first job.
She raised the worry early on
that everything felt off
about the clever ways that they
devised to waste our days
through urgent little tasks we did
with stormy-mind malaise.

The Rules, though I believe you know,
are mostly "play pretend" —
you make believe your boss is smart,
your colleague is your friend.
Then act like you were born to write
the emails they ignore,
and tell yourself you make enough
to leave life at the door.

But she would not obey The Rules —
instead she wore her truth —
and when they saw she would not play
they blamed it on her youth.
They told her she would have to learn
to wear a faker face
to shut her mouth and nod along
in their made-up play-place.

And when they could not tame the mare
that kicked away her reign
they walked her out the door and said
"This causes us such pain!"
But in the space she left behind
I heard them make a toast
"To our control!" they clinked and clapped,
"The thing that matters most!"

Now she's the butt of every joke
in broken break room chat
The kid who wouldn't play her role:
"That loud, unruly brat!"
But sometimes, on those quiet days,
I'll think of her and sigh
and feel The Rules around my neck
as my life wanders by.

SUMMER IN SILICON VALLEY

As June presents her hottest days
I watch you falter through the haze
as you pull down the window shade
and let this blooming summer fade

you, engineer without a train;
you, scientist not yet insane;
you, kid who sought to pierce the sky
now peer through windows' light and sigh

each office day is dark roast buzz
that makes your mind go pixel-fuzz
you stack your paper edges neat
and dream that someday you'll retreat

to sprawl upon a breezy beach
to sip on something cold, light, sweet
to know that it was worth the time:
this daily drag; this metered grind.

Until that future sunny day
you'll file Junes like this away
to arch your heart above a screen
and code the modern West Coast dream.

ADHD

I'll sometimes place a pinkened fingertip upon my brow
and with apology I'll shake my head:
"Too many tabs are open here," I gingerly avow,
"and some are playing music. Please, repeat what you just said" —

— at 25 I learned that I'm alternatively wired,
so rapid notions circle like a swarm,
and there are those who gather thoughts like kindling for a fire
while I am chasing twigs as they go dancing in a storm —

— and when I was 15 I had an infamous high score
of tardiness and deadlines overdue.
They said "You're so creative but your focus is so poor!
We're very disappointed when you choose to not come through" —

— but they could never see that I was clinging to the ship
as seismic shutters spun me to the fray.
My brain will either seize a thought in toothy lockjaw grip
or go spaghetti-strainer stunned and let things fall away —

— but should you ever ask if I might like to trade my mind,
I'd tense up like a dog about to bite.
Because when my prismatic shattered focus realigns
the top of my head hinges off and out bursts golden light —

— and in these moments I feel so expansively alive.

STRING LIGHTS

When Illinois went glittering white
and afternoons froze into night
my dad and I would don our boots
to dig the mailman out a route,
then excavate a box of lights
to string them up at gutter heights.
My eyes would sting with freezing tears
and he would go red in the ears.
Then mom would light the stove for tea
and we'd go in — my dad and me —
and beam with pride at all we'd done
to make some good of absent sun.

They say I act just like my dad,
my turn-of-phrase; my never-mad;
the stubborn way I'll dig my heel
into the fault of how I feel.
And, honestly, I think they're right
since we both make a dark room bright
by sticking pushpins into time
and wrapping moments into rhyme.
He'll spark a flame with piano keys
while I shed pretty prose like leaves.
Though now we unlock different doors
my bluest mind's eye still adores

the moments we've encased in ice
when we'd create the world with lights.

ON MOTHERS AND MOTHS

It was a common summer open-window
occurrence for a fluffy white moth
to find it's blind way to my childhood room
and anchor itself to the wall.

I recall my mother would bring in a broom.
She spoke of the moth-nibbled fate to befall
our holiday wools and lacy white drapes if we
let the critter roam free.

With glee, the kitties would dance with their
full moon-size eyes underfoot as she
ushered the snowfall-soft moth to
the window and bid it farewell.

I tell you this memory now decades on:
my witch-woman mother who cast like a spell
a resolute sweep of her broomstick to quell
the hint of a threat to her family and where we dwell.

SUMMER IN ATLANTA

We used to puff pass on a weathered brown couch
that we borrowed but never returned. With vinyl chainsmoker songs
played through the night, we leaned Closer in with each burn.

Two floors and five beds with a wooded backyard
where rain sometimes flood to the deck. With mice in the pantry
and landlord: a rat — we toasted Buds praising the wreck.

The eight of us lived there — five guys and three girls —
wet counters and floors left unswept. The door was unlocked
so our friends and friends' friends could let themselves in as we slept.

We lit up the grill every night that July,
cracked beers in our flip flops and shorts. We poured sticky shots
and sang into the sky, like horns on ships passing near ports.

Foreverness then seemed as wide as the sky;
time crept in like kudzu and mint. Glass bottles and pipes
echoed ever of us — that human, ebullient sprint.

Now five years have passed and I live on my own.
I wind down for bed around ten. Still, some summer nights
when the wind blows just so, I think of those dim 1AMs.

DEAR PROFESSOR

Dear Professor J—
It's me! The student you advised.
I'm writing to inform you of
some things I've realized. You may recall
for years I sought your mentorship like gold.
But last we spoke about careers, you creased
your brow and told

this wide-eyed girl it was not smart
for me to stay my course. That I
should give up on this art like putting down
a horse. You told me I would not succeed,
the skills were just not there, and
likely not a soul would read
my writing. It is rare

to know it in the moment that your life's
about the change. It happened
in slow motion — like the walls all rearranged,
and shadows on your owl face
became all long and strange. You had
the measured, pitied grace of
drowning cats with mange.

I think the worst part of it all was
how I held back tears and thanked you,
hunching over small with shoulders
to my ears. And then I took into the world
the weight of what you said. I found the
black pit of my soul and dropped my dreams
down dead.

A year went by, then two, then three — I
did not touch the pen. My writing
bachelor's degree became a
wasted spend. I cuffed myself to email chains
and rusty board reports, developed
phantom shoulder pains and
sought out last resorts.

I gnawed upon the bones of time
and let life pass me by. My days lacked
meaning, meter, rhyme so I tried
not to try. Until, about a year ago,
I really hit the floor and there I lay
decaying slow. I shriveled to the core.

Then in that very darkest night,
beneath a coat of grime, I caught a
glimmered glimpse of light concealed
beneath your crime. With rotten hands
I cleared debris to get a better look, and
dizzy, nauseous, cautiously I pulled loose
what you took.

Professor J, I was a kid.
The world was mine to earn. Yet you
trapped me inside a grid and thought
me yours to burn. I felt my hollow body
fall upon the painful truth that
I had such potential in my dreamy,
boundless youth.

I screamed and let the colors fly
from out between my ribs,
then doubled over in a cry and
pressed my bloody lips
upon the cracking crown of who I
dreamed that I could be. Then all around
me pealed the sound of poems breaking free.

So that's what brings me back to here—
this poem that I wrote. I'm setting myself
free this year like scraping off a coat. Professor J,
I must insist I make a bold request.
I have your guidance with me now,
but I think it'd be best

If I could pack it in a box
and send it back to you. Reuse it,
toss it to the rocks — I don't care what you do,
but either way it's no good here —
in fact it never was. I think
I only let it steer my life
so long because

it's easier to run and hide from
that which you love most, and
if you never really try you'll always
have its ghost. Regardless, now I curl my hands
into the fertile earth, and one by one
I'm rooting up new poems ripe with mirth.

Now after all this time I'm sure
you've long forgotten me, but
if you ever read these words
I hope you come to see
that you did not have any right to
prune my budding dream, and I am
weaving words in spite
of your malicious scheme

to craft a world where men like you
block out the young and loud.
I'm pushing now to pave a path
to that which you once shroud.
So now that I've untangled you
from who I'd like to be, I'm off
to see this future through!

Sincerely,
Emily

TOP BUNK

You have taken my lungs
and my teeth and my tongue—

my guts and my spine
and my I-I-I—

I'm all damp and bright red
and you, you usurper—

My sunset, your gold head
(and he, the horizon—)

You are sinking out of sight.

You, who did suck your fingers
on the bunk bed beneath me—

whose hair I did cut
to the kitchen floor—

whose nose I did kiss
as it pinkened in the schoolyard winter—

you are orange, fading fast
to a starry blackened bruise.

2017

BUTTERFLY NET

In garden beds of golden green
my sister and I could be seen
in lion's crouch with kitten eyes
awaiting wayward butterflies.

The dewy drippy summer air
wove sunspark glimmers in her hair
and on my porcelain freckled nose
I burned the pink of winter rose.

When I was six and she was five,
still learning how to be alive,
we'd sometimes argue what was fair
when we had just one net to share.

I felt such loss when I'd defer
the butterflies that flew to her.
It's difficult to see what's real
when at the whim of how you feel.

Our butterfly net-wielding days
were prologue to the ashfall grays
when she and I would scream and break
our spines along the coal-hot rake

of bloody-knuckle feud untamed
for one man's love we both had claimed.
The man was mine before they met,
but they collided and she whet

his interest — and my sister was
drawn in by that electric buzz
of being that which someone sought.
Their secret spread like crimson rot.

So that began the chapter where
we kept no sisterhood to share
nor sportsmanship; with weapons drawn
we set flame to our Parents' lawn.

I scorched the earth beneath her bed,
she flayed my heartbox ruby red,
our splintered ribs broke pearly skin,
and we threw off the bond of kin.

When we had nothing more to lose
We turned to him and thundered "CHOOSE!"
He looked at me with thoughtful eyes,
came close and, much to my surprise,

cut loose the thread that kept us tied
and shuffled me off to the side,
then pulled her in and touched her cheek.
I swore that I would never speak

to her again for what she stole.
I filled a wine glass poison-full,
tore out my teeth and cut my hair
and spat up crimson blood, ensnared

until I felt as good as dead
and all my friends had long since fled.
Then, Lady Lazarus, I rose
with bony fingers, broken toes.

I cut my peach-pit Georgia life
to bite-size pieces with a knife,
then dug my fingers in the earth
and crowned myself into new birth

like bursting forth from some cocoon
I shook my wet new wings and soon
departed from that hollowed me —
my eyes cast high, my shoulders free.

The caterpillar, too, must crawl
upon the earth, and she must fall
into that metamorphic dive
before she's able to arrive

upon the doorstep of her soul
and drink until she's nectar-full —
such was the fertile ground from which
I grew a life nutrient-rich.

My sister and I took three years
to dry our ringing, stinging tears.
The man was gone — a passing cloud
that left our homeland darkness-shroud.

We knelt together in the dirt
and let ourselves behold the hurt
of having fought a fraughtless war
when all we wanted, at our core,

was to repair some deep-held dearth
of our sense of inherent worth.
When you are young your heart is set
on catching selfhood with a net.

We had to learn it's not out there,
it doesn't float by on the air,
but rather lives within our bones
and only we could roll the stones

of self-assigned effacing hate
that threatens to control our fate.
With this great human curse undone,
there's nothing for us to outrun —

— and now that we've disarmed that gun,
again, we're sisters in the sun.

CAESURA

How Ethereal:
to peer beyond the rocky ledge
of who you were, who you will be;
to break your ties and dive into
your shrouded second act;

to burst forth choking
breathless, soaking, shaking
newborn pink, and
press your forehead down upon
the promise of wet ink

Now Seeking: Sense of Self

feat. The Street Philosopher

WHO AM I?!

When I was 22, I had an IDENTITY CRISIS

I had just graduated + moved to Boston,

Come home, I don't know what to do by myself.

But I'm at work...

where the only person I knew was my boyfriend,

☑ get into college
☑ get good grades
☑ direct a play
☑ plan a fundraiser
☑ apply to honors program
☑ enter student film contest

and I was accustomed to putting my time + energy toward external objectives.

☑ graduate

Naturally, the newfound freedom to do whatever I wanted was

Overwhelming

HELP! I'm drowning in a sea of ENDLESS POSSIBILITY!

I didn't know where to go next...

Freelance
office job
Grad School

I became afraid that my entire identity was like a mirror—

0,0

—reflective of those around me but

I started asking strangers for guidance...

... desperately hoping I'd bump into a sense of direction.

One of those strangers was

The Street Philosopher

(a friend of local Boston legend, Mr. Not Art)

Everyone was welcome to sit with them on the sidewalk—

—and I asked:

— so I sat —

How do I find my authentic self? What is my identity independent of external influence?

Part 2

WHEN WINTER BREAKS

I'd come to accept the barren trees:
spindly and reaching;
black corners somberly etching the sheet of the sky.
Remember how we lamented the tragic landscape
as we drove bleary-eyed to
office, apartment, groceries and over again?
The blues of my eyes went
gray like the storms greeting
us every morning alarm.

Cool glass, quiet nights, dark days,
moments lost like notes in the grooves
of a skipping record —
Eternally desolate drear
puddled quiet and still...

Until...

Like the spring of a bud on a new pepper plant,
the first ray of sun burst forth
unannounced from the clouds, and we
stumbled like drunkards so
breathlessly back to ourselves.

The world went emerald-eyed overnight:
hungry for the sprawling sky,
warm to its sun-dried core,
and we — the briefly human —
took to the streets as though heralding end to the war.

We cast up the floodlights that lived in our hearts
toward billowing blue and filled ourselves full
with a shimmering gold that rolled
from the late afternoon and lovingly into the eve.
Back and forth we all beamed
with a hand-holding warmth, and
sky-wide like fireworks spoke with our eyes
the promise that this lovely world was all as it should be.

(*We said:*)
The high for today is Now!
And Now!
And (once again) Now!

I DON'T MISS YOU —

— in the bathwater pools
of my up-at-night mind
sinking into the black
where my bare feet will land
on the splintering floor
deep inside —

(— and I think
that I wish you were here.)

The sadness was our food. On
Wednesday nights we'd gorge ourselves
with cakey despair letting
salty trails streak down our chins.
We'd choke with delight on how
deep we could let ourselves sink.

I SEE YOU I'd say so that
you'd say it back. We'd grip hands
and dive headfirst into the
churn of the sea where our hollowed-out
peach-pits would rattle like something alive.

Then we'd howl at the sun
when the 5am bus
would go grumbling by;
our night-time forever
snatched cruelly from under
our feet.

We'd topple headfirst to the
hard-sharpened edge of the day —

— then shoulder our suffering
souls and proceed on our way.

POET GIRL'S PRAYER

Wide-eyed poet girl, are you so sad?

You claim you'd like to save the world —
but you're on hands and knees
obsessing over things that you once had.
Let the hurt unfurl. Can it be all that bad?

Side-eyed poet girl, you've got regret

manifesting in the shapes of faces
that belong to names of
those you fear you never will forget.
Look upon the world! That sun has set,

and soon you'll see the scars they left will fade.
Bright-eyed poet lover girls cannot be killed
by words that cut or
those who choose to wield them like a blade.

Pride-eyed poet girl, don't be afraid.

And tie-dyed poet girl, you are so real —
real and raw and out of reach from
those who try to tell you that
from which you are and aren't allowed to heal.

Wide-eyed poet girl, trust what you feel.

I FORGIVE YOU, STRANGER

Saturday quiet: sock-foot and placid.
Pearled white light unfurls in
like the jacket of a stranger
sat beside me on a full flight.
I forgive you, stranger.
Let us share the space.

In some teetered tip of cosmic connection —
some skittering neuron nervously navigating
the overgrown gardens of my mind —
your thorny image conjures.

Here, safe, I regard you like wreckage,
not with loathing as I long have,
nor with fear like I felt before that. Only
idle supposing; fleeting awareness that you, too,
are passing through this Saturday in
some uncertain where.

We dangle here a moment; then
I reel back in my breath, and you dissolve
again to fertile ground.

There.

Now if we have to inventory
rights and wrongs in death, you no longer can claim
that, in my poems, you're not found.

SPILT

i.
You spill a glass of water as a last resort.
The table jumps. A critic spits your name.
Your sister's amber-still.

They (your sister) had been caught in the brute,
brusque crush of your grandfather's grip. He's a dog
with a toy, demanding to know the details of
who they are dating.

ii.
On the car ride home, your pants are still wet. Your sister
slumps forward — tea-set fragile, sparrow small. A critic
sets his glasses upon the tip of his nose and reads

his scathing review: "We should have seen it coming.
We should have had a plan for how we tell grandpa
about her whole situation." He speaks like he's
setting a table on their wingless back.

iii.
Months later, over the phone, you ask
your sister if they remember that day, and
they are audibly wincing. They sigh that they wish
they did not have to hide (and hide from) who they love.

The line goes quiet and taut. You hear in that space all the sunsets
and night-breaking sunrises they've had to shed.
"I'm sorry," you say
(as if it could make up for years of the sorrys unsaid)

BREATH

Umbilical cord between body and mind —
a moment that touches your teeth.

A flavorful broth and a fruit on the vine —
a gown you can wear but can't keep.

It rubs like a cat on the yawn of your ribs —
then shakes off its shape and departs.

It winds on the wind breaking free from your lips —
then always another one starts.

I FORGIVE YOU, LOVER

We fight on the foreboding edge
of a summer moon's glow. You speak
in staccato to accent your sense
of vexation with what we now sow.

You say something harsh; something
sharpened by loveless rough edges of people
we were — by years of the joined
and disjointed ways we've healed and hurt.

I forgive you, Lover

I know it is hard to be here in a garden
so verdant and canopy-blue, but to know
underfoot there are roots and red soot
from the summers where you and I grew.

HALF MOON BAY

The coming-in of night
is not a gentle thing:

the weighted blanket of dusk; thick, blue, wet;
asphalt a patchwork of rain.

We eye the ground for fumbling newts
as trees puff crepuscular breath.

The wind rips but it's playful:
free to rumble, unbound, indigo,

eager and tugging with bracing ebullience
into a crescent-shaped dark.

THE VINTAGE SHOP

One daisy yellow autumn you and I wore button coats
and strolled to pick up cold brew down the road.
Your sleeve of weathered herringbone bore shades of spice rolled oats,
and on my boots were faded spots from last year when it snowed.

Like alley cats we wandered over streets of cobblestone
while winter's wind foreshadowed through my hair.
We stopped outside a vintage shop and, frozen to the bone,
took temporary shelter in the store among its ware.

Inside were rows of crystal cups and floral painted plates,
a velvet couch which looked to be well-sat,
a willow tree of crosses, rusty pair of leather skates,
and sprawled across a stack of bags: a tabby sleep-eyed cat.

And though we'd only come inside for cover from the cold
a fascinated glimmer lit my eye.
I've always had a tenderness for things well-used and old
that lend themself to wonderings of those they were loved by.

So as you checked your phone I took a lap around the shop
and touched my finger lightly to the goods.
I pondered how each trinket might have shown up as a prop
for scenes of love and loss and long-gone won'ts and woulds and shoulds.

But when I paused to pet the cat I stole a glance your way
to find your loving eyes were set on me.
Your hands were in your pockets and your eyebrows rose to say
that when you find me lost in thought you know to let me be.

Returning to your side I reeled your hand back into mine
And wordless, we continued on our path.
Perhaps one day we'll join the rank of stories lost to time
but in the joyful now we'll face the wind and all its wrath.

NEIGHBOR BOY

"We were born to be good friends, Anne.
You've thwarted destiny long enough."

— Gilbert Blythe, *Anne of Green Gables*

If they took samples of our brains and test results came back
informing us we're psychopaths, I think we'd shrug and laugh.

I'd set the world ablaze for you. I'd drive into the haze for you.
I'd let my bones and pink sinew unscrew, and I would dive into
a churning sea of green and blue should you be wading water too —
We'll craft a raft made from *I do* and see this tragic life thing through.

You tip your starry hips into the linens of our bed
and hold me in the folding of your arms.
You press your earthy lips into the crown upon my head
and I go spinning moony-eyed entangled in your charms.

We've lived so many lives but we were always side by side:
you neighbor boy; you academic foe.
I've seen you on your hands and knees: a victim of your pride.
I've seen you with blood in your teeth. I've heard your loudest crow.

And when I trace the winding steps to where it all began —
to when your parents moved in next to mine —
I see my child self observing you like newfound land.
She watches from the window pane. (She thinks that you look kind.)

Now seven years I've made our bed and toasted you your morning bread
and kissed your sleepy dreamy head and one day, when we both are dead,
I'll turn to face you in the dark — disrupt your slumber like lark
to place my hand upon your heart and ask — What was your favorite part?

It's us insane conceited two here in the garden that grew
and since it all began I knew that I'd collide with you.
(*I do.*)

WHAT IF THIS IS ALL WE GET?

The crisp morning light
This little apartment
The fresh, sweet-smelling
strawberries that you are
slicing with care.

What if forever really has a
beginning and end, and when
our flame flickers out we
disperse to the air and
dissolve back into the earth?

What if I can't bring you with me?
And this living room dance,
intertwined fingers, warm hips and hands,
soft moonlit glow, forehead to lips —
What if that's it?

If that were the case I'd have no other choice
than to lay with my head on your chest;
to wade through the soft ocean roll
of your rise-and-fall breath — then joyfully toss
on the waves of the moments we get.

DEAR GOVERNOR

I hope this poem finds you well and
your day's not too full! I'm reaching
out with interest in applying for the role of
Poet Laureate in California. You will find
my skills and my professional
ambitions are aligned!

I did not see an application
portal on your site
where up-and-coming laureates
could easily apply.
So I thought reaching out to you
might be the quickest way

to let you know I'm interested
and I can start today. I'm sure
that you'll be wondering
what's setting me apart
from all the other candidates —
please find attached my heart!

I'm sad to say I'm not a fit
for any other job —
in offices I tend to either chat
too much or sob —
but when I'm writing poems
I can feel my fingers burn,

the top of my head floats away
and all my doubts adjourn. It's like
I come back to myself and cry
"Oh there you are!" and
then I catch my soft pink soul
inside a mason jar.

But doubtless now you're asking me
what's in the deal for you? I'm sure
it's an important role in keeping
our state true to our most honest selves
and building bridges through the blue
of atmospheric rivers of the mind that tend to brew.

Dear Governor, I promise I can
catch the people's ears by walking on the
tightrope line between our hopes and fears
and I can do a little spin and catch the crowd
off-guard, and I'll remind them all to breathe
as you work very hard

to douse the wild fires dancing on
our country's stage, where endless news
of suffering keeps us in constant rage. As
Poet Laureate I know I might not save the earth,
but while you work on that I'll shepherd
spirits to the hearth.

I'm grateful for your time as you consider
my request. If I could say just one more thing:
I'm not yet at my best! But if you trust me
with this role I promise I will grow to fill
the shoes of all the poets past
who ran the show.

And if you'd like to chat over a coffee
I'll drop by! And if it's not my year I hope
you'll keep my name in mind. But either way
I'm pleased we could connect to this degree.
I'll keep a watch for your response.

Sincerely,
Emily

BUILDING A NEST

I am building a nest for myself in my heart
with sticky bits and feathery bobs.
I scale its edge with spidery steps to
weave a trapeze of dreams.

I use what I can find: poems and pretty words;
a crimson clever turn of phrase;
tomato vines of blush and blaze.
My fingers trace the fraying ends
of notes I wrote but did not send,
and things never said, and fear of the dead—
all wrapped in a bow of urgent ambitions.
I hang a hat of regret near the doorway
of a daydream into which I dare not peek.

I am building a nest for myself in my heart.
From such a perch I overlook all I am —
and from here there's a clear and continuous path
that lets out just near the place I am trying to go.

SAVASANA

Bring awareness back to your body

as though it were water.
As though you have carried it, sputtering,
up a rocky hill in the hollow
cup of your palms.

Press it up to the smooth bony ledge of your brows

then unlatch your shoulders. Crack your chest open
the way a chick shatters an egg. Angle your crown
up and back in search of the hesitant tug of rubbery bands
connecting the stretch of soft space from your collar to chin

and hold how you've strung up your stories like beads on a string —

minutes and months make a bread-crumby trail to the place
that you're now calling you. The incomprehensible present;
the disposable, irreplaceable now. When you set your sight
on a non-moving point, you fasten your mind to the moment;

your flurry of thoughts will stay stuck to the back of your eyes.

You steal from your selfness when leaning against
the cool window glass of the world. Shut the shades
of your eyes and refer back to you. This is your home.
You are your home.

Now be in your body and breathe.

PRETTY THINGS

Fill your life with pretty things
like store bouquets and copper rings

Make a bed of things that squish
and drape your hips with things that swish

Paint the walls an eggshell blue
and grocery shop in high heel shoes

Dive head first into the sea
and carve your name into a tree

Cut your hair the way you like
as you enjoy a morning hike

Kiss your neighbor on the lips
then drink your tea in little sips

Frost a cake with lemon cream
and drift into a midday dream

Pop champagne on Wednesday night
or challenge someone to a fight

Call a friend to just say hi
and publish your own book — or try!

String your words like wooden beads
and scatter sweet ideas like seeds

Bright the night with lights on strings —
and let yourself unclip your wings.

Notice all the joy it brings.
(Your life can be a pretty thing!)

ACKNOWLEDGEMENTS

Creative projects like this are nourished by the support and celebration of our communities. I am extremely fortunate to have had the love and encouragement of my friends and family throughout this summer-long book writing and publishing project. I am grateful to my mother and sister for being my first readers and editors – and equally grateful to my partner, former neighbor, and spelling bee competitor Gustavo for reading each poem in its first unpolished and handwritten draft.

Thank you to my friends and early readers Frankie, Meg, and Kate, my Downtown San Jose yoga community, and the wonderful humans who cheered me on throughout this project on Instagram. Thank you to the artist who helped bring "Butterfly Net" into the visual world, Maria Ananieva. For the wisdom and guidance that helped lead me to writing this book, I am very grateful to my father, to Mr. Not Art and his Street Philosopher friend, as well as the countless friends who stepped in to help when I most needed it – including Ruth, Scott, Shannon, Barrie, Katie, Karen, Tori, Kayleigh, Daron, Yang, Charlotte, Kailes, and Jill.